How to Discover
the Will of God

How to Discover the Will of God

by
George Sweeting

World Wide
P U B L I C A T I O N S
A ministry of the Billy Graham Association

1303 Hennepin Avenue
Minneapolis, Minnesota 55403

Library of Congress Cataloging in Publication Data

Sweeting, George, 19xx-
　How to Discover the Will of God.

　1. Social ethics.　2. Christian ethics.　3. Social problems.
　I. Title.
HM216.R95　　　　　170　　　　　81-16804
ISBN 0-8024-3633-1

Paperback Edition, 1982

11 12 Printing/LC/Year 88 87 86 85 84

Printed in the United States of America

This book is affectionately dedicated to
HERRMANN GEORGE BRAUNLIN
*who has pastored the Hawthorne Gospel
Church of Hawthorne, New Jersey
for over fifty years to the glory of God.*

Contents

1

God's Way Is the Best Way

"I am come that they might have life, and that they might have it more abundantly" *(John 10:10).*

"Wherefore be ye not unwise, but understanding what the will of the Lord is" *(Ephesians 5:17).*

"Not with eyeservice, as menpleasers; but as the servants of Christ, doing the will of God from the heart" *(Ephesians 6:6).*

"Epaphras, who is one of you, a servant of Christ, saluteth you, always labouring fervantly for you in prayers, that ye may stand perfect and complete in all the will of God" *(Colossians 4:12).*

"Teach me thy way, O Lord, *and lead me in a plain path" (Psalm 27:11).*

"I delight to do thy will, O my God: *yea thy law is within my heart" (Psalm 40:8).*

1

God's Way Is the Best Way

We are living in troubled times!

It is impossible to predict from one day to the next what the morning headlines will announce. In this day of international tension and political confusion, it is very easy to wonder if there are any certainties in life at all. Is anyone in control? Does anyone have the answers?

The Bible answers with a resounding

yes! For the child of God there is a better way. There is light in darkness, there is reason amidst confusion. There is a path to follow!

One of the most thrilling realities in all of life is the realization that God has a *plan* for your life! That's right! God has a plan, a design for every one of us. And when we discover that plan—then, and only then, can we find true meaning and an eternal purpose for our existence.

Some time ago the construction of the gigantic Sears Tower was officially completed in the city of Chicago. It is a magnificent sight, stretching nearly fifteen hundred feet into the sky! The moment a person looks at this impressive building he is immediately reminded of the tremendous amount of work and development that went into its construction. For years plans were made and blueprints were drawn. Endless engineering research was undertaken so that this magnificent structure could become a reality. Why? Because buildings do not just happen. They require a plan.

The very same principle is true with you, my friend. The puzzle of life will never be put together without the direction that only God can give. The pieces do not just fall in place. There must be order and design. One must follow God's blueprint!

Many people today seem to be wandering about in a fog. They are groping from one day to the next trying to find the magic formula—the key that will open the door to fulfillment and purpose. They never seem to know which way to turn, yet they appear willing to follow anyone and try anything.

The world is a kind of spiritual kindergarten where bewildered infants are trying to spell God with the wrong blocks.

Edwin Arlington Robinson

Not long ago a French author produced a novel with unbound, unnumbered pages. The reader was expected first to shuffle all the pages and then to read the story that resulted. This aimlessness may seem wild, but for multitudes today, life itself appears just as senseless. Why, they ask, does it matter which page comes last, first, or in the middle? In a very real sense, man has lost his way. According to one psychologist's analysis of events, the present generation is "out of touch with its being and thus out of touch with God." Emptiness, confusion, aimlessness, and loneliness abound.

I cannot find my way: there is no star
In all the shrouded heavens any-
* where.*

Edwin Arlington Robinson
"Credo"

As I see him, the unutterably infin-
itesimal individual weaves among the

mysteries a floss-like and wholly mean-ingless course—if course it be. In short, I catch no meaning from all I have seen and pass quite as I came, confused and dismayed.

Theodore Dreiser
What I Believe

But life does not have to be like that! Jesus said, "I am come that they might have life, and that they might have it more abundantly" (John 10:10). God's plan for each one of us is that we have a full, exciting, purposeful, and abundant life! It makes a great deal of sense that the God who is the master Designer, the Creator and Sustainer of the universe, should also be interested in the plan of our lives. He who hung the worlds in space *must* be concerned about us, His creation.

In his book, *The Perfect Will of God,* G. Christian Weiss asks,

Can you think of a father who has no

will or plan for the life of his son? Can you imagine a mother who has no clear will or definite ambition for her daughter? Can you imagine a man who has no special desire or pattern in the one he choses to be his wife? Can you conceive of a king or ruler who has no will or desire or law to govern the conduct of his people? A captain who has no plan for his soldiery? An employer who has no plan or pattern to guide the labor of his workers? If so, then you may also think that God does not have a plan for your life, for every one of these symbols is used in the Bible to represent the relation the Christian bears to his Lord.

With the dawning of the Age of Reason and the scientific approach to knowledge, there arose in the eighteenth century the philosophy of deism. This was the belief that although God did create the universe, He had abandoned the world and left it to be governed by natural law. God became an "absentee God" no longer interested in His creation.

But look for a moment at what the Bible has to say about that. The apostle

Peter wrote that the Lord "is longsuffering to us-ward, not willing that any should perish, but that all should come to repentance" (2 Peter 3:9). Paul assured us, "God, who [on many occasions] and in [various ways] spake in time past unto the fathers by the prophets, hath in these last days spoken unto us by his Son" (Hebrews 1:1). God is interested in us. He has provided for our salvation, and He wants each of us to experience the meaning and satisfaction of His will for our lives.

Unfortunately, many people today neglect or refuse to accept God's plan for their lives. They want to run their own show, make all their own moves. They refuse to let God have control. The result is turmoil, uncertainty, futility, and often chaos.

Why is it important to accept God's plan for your life? Here are four reasons why God's way is not only the best way, but ultimately the only way to find lasting purpose for living.

———————◆———————

1. *You need to know God's will because only God knows the future.*

There is an enormous interest today in

trying to look into the future. Nearly fifteen hundred newspapers across this country print daily horoscope columns. Millions of people, many well-known people, openly confess that they plan their day's activities only after they have consulted the stars. Hundreds of self-professed witches may be found in every part of the United States, holding seances and dispensing psychic counsel. Famous seers and so-called prophets are selling books by the millions to readers who are hungry for some insight into tomorrow. Determining the future has become a national obsession.

But the Bible says that it is foolish for us to try to peer into the future. Proverbs 27:1 warns, "Boast not thyself of tomorrow; for thou knowest not what a day may bring forth." Isaiah spoke the words of Jehovah, saying, "I am God, and there is none like me, declaring *the end from the beginning,* and from ancient times *the things that are not yet done*" (Isaiah 46:9-10). Many people may make predictions concerning the future, some may guess correctly some of the time, others may appear to have extrasensory powers—but no one can give you a complete picture of what will happen tomorrow. No one knows the future but God!

We do not know what lies ahead; only God does. Job declared, "He knoweth the way that I take" (Job 23:10). We must find God's will and follow in His way because He alone is able to lead us through the uncertainties of tomorrow. No matter how dark the clouds of life may appear, the Lord knows, and He cares, and He will lead us through the storms if we walk with Him.

I know not, but God knows;
Oh, blessed rest from fear!
All my unfolding days
To Him are plain and clear
Each anxious puzzled "Why?"
From doubt or dread that grows,
Finds answer in this thought:
I know not, but He knows.

I cannot but God can;
Oh, balm for all my care!
The burden that I drop

His hand will lift and bear,
Though eagle pinions tire,—
I walk where once I ran,
This is my strength to know:
I cannot, but God can.
Annie Johnson Flint

2. You need to accept God's will because only God knows what is best for you.

One of the greatest mysteries of life is that although most of us know what we *like* and what we *want*, we are often completely mistaken as to what we *need* or what is *best* for our lives.

I am sure there are many people who would hardly recognize God's will or guidance if it were shown to them, because all they are looking for is God's blessing on their own plans. What they need is not for God to give them their requests, but to experience a complete change in their motives and desires. God is not interested in putting His stamp of approval on *our* actions. He longs to guide us into *His* purpose and plan.

Now, that does not mean that He will necessarily make us do things we do not want to do. God knows us far better than we know ourselves. He wants us to be happy, to enjoy life. But He also knows that we are incapable of planning our lives. We do not always know what is best or what will bring the greatest peace and fulfillment.

"In His will is our peace."
Dante

It is very strengthening to realize that God is more concerned than we are that we know His will. Because of sin, our desire to know and obey God's way is weakened. The epistle of James tells us that often it is *indecision* rather than *wrong decisions* that defeats us. We have

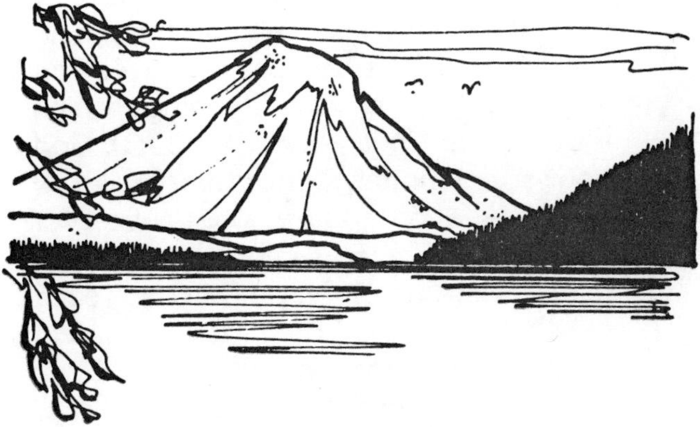

not because we ask not. We are compared to a double-minded man who is "unstable in all his ways" (James 1:8). We need to acknowledge, like the prophet Jeremiah, that we are totally incapable of charting our own course. "O LORD," cried Jeremiah, "I know that the way of man is not in himself: it is not in man that walketh to direct his steps" (Jeremiah 10:23).

God honored that humble prayer and promised to lead Jeremiah in the way that he should take. "Call unto me," said the Lord, "and I will answer thee, and shew thee great and mighty things, which thou knowest not" (Jeremiah 33:3). God knows us infinitely better than we know ourselves, and He knows what is best for our lives. With the psalmist, we should pray, "Shew me thy ways, O LORD; Teach me thy paths. Lead me in thy truth, and teach me: for thou art the God of my salvation; on thee do I wait all the day" (Psalm 25:4-5).

I have visited some of the great, historic churches of Christendom. Often the stained-glass windows of these churches look very dull and uninteresting from the outside. But what a startling difference when one looks at the windows from the inside; they are not dull, but dynamic, dazzling, and beautiful. Many times God's will may appear dark and difficult, until you step inside His will. Then you suddenly discover that God really knows what is best for us.

3. *You need to know God's will because God has a plan of blessing just for you.*

Is your life all that you want it to be? Are you experiencing the abundant kind of living Jesus came to bring? You can, you know.

Many people today think it is foolish to believe that God is personally interested in each one of us. "In this day of giant computers and space travel," they say, "how would God be interested in me? I am just one little speck in this vast universe!"

Man is an inhabitant of a thin rind on a negligible detached blob of matter, be-

longing to one of the millions of stars, in one among millions of island universes.
H. G. Wells

But the Bible teaches that though we are frail and insignificant in many ways, we are created in the image of God. We are fearfully and wonderfully made. No, we are not meaningless accidents who have been thrust into time and space. We are the special creation of a God who cares. Though we have sinned and the image of God in us has been defaced, salvation is possible through the sacrifice of Jesus Christ on the cross. The news of the gospel is that God has for you *a plan of blessing* that began in eternity past and stretches on forever.

God spoke to Jeremiah and said, "Before I formed thee . . . I knew thee; and before thou camest forth . . . I sanctified thee, and I ordained thee a prophet unto the nations" (Jeremiah 1:5). God's plan and purpose for each one of us was designed and ordained before the world even began. What a colossal tragedy to miss out on such a breathtaking plan! What a waste of God's wisdom, talent, and love not to appropriate all that He has for us!

The apostle Paul taught, "We are [God's] workmanship [handiwork], created in Christ Jesus unto good works, which God hath before ordained that we should walk in them" (Ephesians 2:10). I shall never, never forget the day when it dawned on me that the infinite God had a plan of blessing for my life. I bowed my head and humbly prayed, "O Lord, I am sorry for the wasted years, forgive me for all the mistakes of the past, and help me to live in the circle of your will."

It is difficult to steer a parked car, so get moving.

Henrietta Mears

Yes, God has an eternal purpose just for you—a divine plan that will bring blessing, fullness, and eternity into your daily life. Do you know that purpose?

4. *You need to know the will of God because God commands us to know and obey His will!*

There is none quite so hopeless as a Christian who refuses to acknowledge God's working in his life. Jonah is a classic example of a man who would not obey the will of God. God told Jonah to go to Nineveh and preach repentance, but he refused. God's will for Jonah was that he be an instrument to reveal God's message and reach a people for Himself.

But what did Jonah do? He turned his back on God. He consciously disobeyed the will of God and sailed off in the opposite direction. And because of his disobedience, God had to judge Jonah. He had to put him in a place where he would be willing to listen, a place where he would obey. Finally Jonah realized that God's way is the best and only way.

Paul told the church at Ephesus not to

be unwise, but "understanding what the will of the Lord is" (Ephesians 5:17). Yes, God commands us to know His will. This is just as much an imperative as any other of the commands of Scripture but how often we fail to obey the will of God. God requires that we obey His will, but He also desires that we obey willingly. Paul wrote again to the Ephesians and said, "As the servants of Christ, [do] the will of God from the heart" (Ephesians 6:6). We are to obey God's will, willingly and completely.

"If ye be willing and obedient, ye shall eat the good of the land" (Isaiah 1:19)

The story is told of the great composer, Felix Mendelssohn, visiting a German cathedral to see a new organ. It was in his early life, and though his music was well known, he was not. When he arrived at

the cathedral, he found the young organist practicing. It so happened that the young man was playing one of Mendelssohn's own pieces. Mendelssohn walked up to the organist and, without introducing himself, requested to play the new instrument. The young organist refused, saying that he did not allow any strange hands to touch this keyboard.

Mendelssohn lingered for a brief moment and then wandered about the sanctuary. However, in a little while he returned and asked, "My friend, will you allow me to play just a little?"

The young organist was angered and asked Mendelssohn to leave the building, saying, "No inexperienced hands dare touch the keyboard of this new organ."

Again, Mendelssohn retreated and even left the sanctuary, but try as he would, he could not go away. His soul was aflame with desire, and he yearned for an opportunity to play the new instrument. For the third time, he returned and said, "My friend, excuse me, but I feel I must ask you once again. Please let me sit down and play the organ, just a little."

Exasperated by his earnestness and persistence, the young organist consented to let him play. Young Mendelssohn sat down and began adjusting the instrument to suit him, while the young organist started to leave the sanctuary. But as soon as Mendelssohn began to play, the young man rushed back to the organ and, looking earnestly at the composer, asked, "Tell me, sir, who are you?"

He said, "My name is Mendelssohn."

"Oh forgive me!" the young organist exclaimed. "I didn't know who you were. Just think, I wouldn't let the master musician take my place and play my instrument!"

Friend, life at best has very little harmony and design. We know very little about how to play on the keyboard of life. And God never intended that we should play it alone. The triune God, God the Father, God the Son, and God the Holy Spirit, gently calls, "Let me direct your life. Let me touch the keyboard, and I'll make music."

Is your life in tune with the will of God? Have you placed your life in the hands of the only One who knows the future? The one who has a plan and purpose just for you? Are you experiencing the joy and

34

harmony that comes from obedience to God's revealed will?

Thy way, not mine, O Lord,
  However dark it be!
Lead me by thine own hand;
  Choose thou the path for me.
Smooth let it be or rough,
  It will be still the best;
Winding or straight, it leads
  Right onward to thy rest.
I dare not choose my lot;
  I would not if I might;
Choose thou for me, my God:
  So shall I walk aright.
Take thou my cup, and it
  With joy or sorrow fill,
As best to thee may seem;
  Choose thou my good and ill.

Choose thou for me my friends,
  My sickness or my health;
Choose thou my cares for me,

My poverty or wealth.
Not mine, not mine the choice,
In things or great or small;
Be thou my guide, my strength,
My wisdom, and my all.
Horatius Bonar

2

How Can I Know God's Will?

"The Lord is not slack concerning his promise, as some men count slackness; but is longsuffering to us-ward, not willing *that any should perish, but that all should come to repentance" (2 Peter 3:9).*

"I beseech you therefore, brethren, by the mercies of God, that ye present your bodies a living sacrifice, holy, acceptable unto God, which is your reasonable service. And be not conformed to this world: but be ye transformed by the renewing of your mind, that ye may prove what is that good, and acceptable, and perfect, will of God" *(Romans 12:1-2).*

"Having made known unto us the mystery of his will, *according to his good pleasure which he hath purposed in himself" (Ephesians 1:9).*

"For this is the will of God, *even your sanctification, that ye should abstain from fornication" (1 Thessalonians 4:3).*

"Forasmuch then as Christ hath suffered for us in the flesh, arm yourselves likewise with the same mind: for he that hath suffered in the flesh hath ceased

from sin; that he no longer should live the rest of his time in the flesh to the lusts of men, but to the will of God" *(1 Peter 4:1-2).*

2

How Can I Know God's Will?

"How can I know God's will for my life?"

That question, probably more than any other, is on the minds and lips of Christians today. "How can I be sure of God's direction in my life?"

Unfortunately, for many people this is a difficult question. "If God has a plan for each person," you ask," why doesn't He reveal it? Can't He show us what He has for us, what He wants us to do?"

The answer is yes, He can! God does have a plan for your life! But He does not usually reveal His lifelong plan for us all at one time. Too many of us think of God's will as some magical blueprint that God lets down from heaven into a person's lap. They are looking for a nice little package that will outline, day by day, each step for the rest of their lives. But God does not usually work that way. He has a plan for you—yes! But He does not want to make you a robot or programmed computer.

First of all, what do we mean by the phrase *the will of God?* In the New Testament there are a number of different words translated as "will" that are used to indicate God's particular plan.

In 2 Timothy 1:9 we read, "Who hath saved us, and called us with an holy calling, not according to our works, but according *to his own purpose* and grace." The word "purpose" here means "to set before oneself." In other words, God set before Himself a plan, and He is now bringing that plan into reality.

In Ephesians 1:9 Paul tells us that this

plan is the result of God's will. "Having made known unto us the mystery of his will, according to his good pleasure which he hath purposed in himself." The word translated "good pleasure" carries the idea, "that which pleases God."

Very simply, God has certain desires in His heart. He decided that it would be wise if these desires were accomplished. Therefore, He has purposed to bring these things to pass. This purpose, and the way in which it is realized, is the will of God.

Second, it is vital to remember that the *will of God* and the Word of God are inseparable.

In his booklet, *Affirming the Will of God,* Paul Little asks, "Has it ever struck you that the vast majority of the will of God for your life has already been revealed in the Bible? That is a crucial thing to grasp." The will of God is directly related to the Word of God.

Throughout the Word of God there are many commands that show us clearly what to do and what not to do. There are yeses and nos. There are positives and negatives. For example, robbery, adul-

tery, and murder are clearly forbidden. We know, for instance, that as fathers we are admonished, "Provoke not your children to wrath: but bring them up in the nurture and admonition of the Lord" (Ephesians 6:4). Or, as believers we are told directly to "be not drunk with wine, wherein is excess; but be filled with the Spirit" (Ephesians 5:18). These are both direct yeses and nos from God, and the Bible is filled with others.

A direct command is an obvious way in which God reveals His will. But what about those areas where the Bible appears to be silent, where there are no direct commands? Where there is no direct, clear teaching on a subject that applies to a particular situation, we are encouraged to seek for scriptural principles. Philippians 2:13 assures us that God "worketh in you both to will and to do of his good pleasure." In other words, God will do His part in communicating His will to us. In 1 Corinthians 2:15-16, the apostle Paul pointed out, "He that is spiritual judgeth all things, yet he himself is judged of no man. For who hath known the mind of the Lord, that he may instruct him? But we have the mind of Christ." Paul was saying that every spiritual person has the divine equipment to make the right decisions.

Surely God is not a celestial dictator who wants to order every movement of our lives. It really makes little difference to him if we drive a Chevy, Ford, Plymouth—or no car at all. He does not wish to tell us what color tie to wear. He is very deeply interested in us, and in all that we do, but He also wants us to use our own sanctified, God-given common sense.

In his article entitled "Four Ways to Find God's Will" (*HIS Magazine*, May 1969), A.W. Tozer has observed,

> *On the surface it might appear more spiritual to seek God's leading than just to go ahead and do the obvious thing. But it isn't. If God gives you a watch, are you honoring Him more by asking Him what time it is or by simply consulting the watch? If God gives a sailor a compass, does the sailor please God more by kneeling in a frenzy of prayer to persuade God to show him which way to go, or should he just steer ahead according to the compass?*

Except for those things that are specifically commanded or forbidden in the Scriptures, it is God's will that we be free to exercise our own intelligent choice. . . . In almost everything that touches our everyday life on earth, God is pleased when we're pleased. He wills that we be as free as birds to soar and sing our Maker's praise without anxiety. God's choice for us may not be only one *but rather any one of a score of possible choices. The man or woman who is* wholly and joyously surrendered to Christ *can't make a wrong choice— any choice will be the right one.*

Sometimes God reveals His will in a definite yes or a dogmatic no. Other times we may be given the opportunity to use our own God-given discernment.

But you ask, "What about the gray areas of life? What about the questions we simply cannot answer? What happens when we have to make a decision, and God has provided no yes, no, or maybe to help us?" At such times we must claim God's promises and simply depend upon the indwelling Holy Spirit to direct us into

His will. David's assurance from God was, "I will instruct thee and teach thee in the way which thou shalt go: I will guide thee with mine eye" (Psalm 32:8). God has promised in His Word that if we trust in Him, He will show us the way to go, He will reveal His will. Solomon wrote in the Proverbs, "Trust in the LORD with all thine heart; and lean not unto thine own understanding. In all thy ways acknowledge him, and he shall direct thy paths" (Proverbs 3:5-6).

Yes, God will show you His will. But remember, you probably will not receive a lifelong blueprint from Him. The Christian life is more of a step-by-step, day-by-day arrangement. God could well direct you all at once into some life's work, or He may lead you just one step at a time. Someone has said that the only way to see far ahead in the will of God is to go ahead just as far as you can see. That is the key, a step-by-step, day-by-day walk with the Lord.

"But how can I know God's will?" you ask. "Is there anything in particular I must do so that He will show me His will in the 'gray' areas of life?"

Although there is no magic formula,

there are several basic prerequisites, specific steps that must be taken before God's will can be known.

Salvation

First and foremost, an individual must be a child of God before he or she can ever hope to know God's will in his life.

God's greatest desire is to be united in fellowship with you and me. Because He "is not willing that any should perish, but that all should come to repentance" (2 Peter 3:9), He sent His Son to die on the cross to provide for our salvation. This is the most significant expression of God's will that you can ever experience. John wrote, "As many as received him, to them gave he power to become the sons of God, even to them that believe on his name: which were born, not of blood, nor of the will of the flesh, nor of the will of man, but of God" (John 1:12-13).

God's will is that we be His children. And until we are born of God He cannot lead us as a father leads his children. He cannot direct us any further in His will. Until we are converted, we can have little part in God's divine plan and purpose.

Have you trusted Jesus Christ as your personal Savior? Have you taken this very first step in the will of God? If not, do it right now. Why not make this your prayer:

Dear Lord, I now understand that all my life I have been running in the wrong direction, away from Your will. I now ask You to turn me around. I believe that You are the only one who can do this. I repent of everything I have done that has displeased You. I believe Jesus Christ died on the cross for my sins. Please forgive me for my sins, adopt me into Your wonderful family, and give me the gift of eternal life with You. From this day on, take over as the only Savior of my life. I want to know and do the will of God. Amen.

Surrender

Second, the Bible points out that it is impossible for us to see further into God's will unless we are willing to obey that will which we have already seen. If you really want God to lead in your life, then you must commit your life to Him.

The condition of an enlightened mind is a surrendered heart.
Alan Redpath

Romans 12:1-2 makes this very clear: "I beseech you therefore, brethren, by the mercies of God, that ye present your *bodies* a living sacrifice, holy, acceptable unto God, which is your reasonable service. And be not conformed to this world: but be ye transformed by the renewing of your *mind,* that ye may prove what is that good, and acceptable, and perfect, *will* of God." The Lord wants our body, our mind, and our will. He bases His appeal on what He has done for us—"by the mercies of God."

The central verb in Romans 12:1 is

"present" or "offer up." This word was commonly used to refer to the act where the owner of the sacrificial victim gives up his victim to the priest for use in the Jewish worship service.

Paul urges every Christian, as a believer-priest (1 Peter 2:9; Revelation 1:6) to offer his entire person, including his body and mind, to God for the purpose of service. Once offered, God accepts, and from then on the person is obligated to perform whatever service or duty is asked by God. Also, from then on God is obligated to deal in a disciplinary manner with that person if he shirks his duty.

Marion H. Nelson
How To Know God's Will

Friend, do you want the good, acceptable, and perfect will of God? The answer is to offer yourself to God in a positive act of surrender. I am convinced that many people are frustrated in their attempt to determine God's will because they are unwilling to yield themselves, to place their lives totally in God's hands.

J. Sidlow Baxter tells of a Christian young woman who had allowed herself to become involved with a young man who was not a believer. The girl's friends, who were very concerned about this relationship, tried their best to tell the young lady that she was heading for trouble. They showed her what the Bible says about being unequally yoked with unbelievers. But the more they talked, it seemed, the more determined she was to have her own way. Finally they got her down on her knees to pray with them, and with emotional gulps she prayed, "Thy will —be done—O Lord—but *please* give me Jimmie!"

God will never lead us to do anything that is contrary to His written Word. Unless we are willing to obey that which we know to be true, we are simply wasting our time in searching for further guidance.

To present your body as a living sacrifice means to be in full, enthusiastic cooperation with God's will. It means to

57

place yourself once and for all upon the altar of God, to affirm *His* purposes and *His* desires in all of life.

I shall never forget my first experience of surrender to Jesus Christ. The messenger God used was Dr. David Otis Fuller. That night as Dr. Fuller spoke, the Holy Spirit called me to begin living a transformed life, to be a transformer rather than a conformer. I wrote down four goals in my Bible that evening:

1. To seek to bring glory to God

2. To cultivate the inner life

3. To disciple as many others as possible

4. To win as many as possible to faith in Jesus Christ

That decision was made many years ago, and I have never forgotten it.

Are you prepared to pay the price to know God's will? Have you taken this step of submission to the lordship of Christ? You will never know all that God has for you until you do. Why not pray with the psalmist right now:

*"I am thy servant; give me under-
standing, that I may know thy tes-
timonies. . . . The entrance of thy
words giveth light; it giveth understanding unto the simple" (Psalm
119:125, 130).*

Separation

Third, God's will can be fully
discovered and understood only by those
with clean hearts and hands. It is God's
will that believers live separated lives. In
1 Thessalonians 4:3, 7, Paul wrote, "For
this is the will of God, even your sanctification. . . . For God hath not called us
unto uncleanness, but unto holiness."

The word *sanctify* means two things:
"to cleanse," and "to set apart." It is the
will of God that we be clean and separated
unto Him.

*We are set apart unto God, in one
sense of the term, the moment we*

receive Christ, for we are bought with the price of His blood. Some day we shall be set apart from sin forever, by being taken to glory with Christ. But 1 Thessalonians 4:3 speaks of our present responsibility. God wants us to take our stand against every form of known sin, and to maintain that stand consistently.

S. Maxwell Coder
God's Will for Your Life

First of all, in 1 Thessalonians 4:3 we are told to "abstain from fornication." That means we are to stay away from sexual sins. The word *abstain* simply means "stay away from." How far away? Far away enough to remain pure. God expects that, as His temple, His abiding place, our bodies are to be pure. God designed sex, and God designed it for the marriage relationship. Sex is good, and sex is beautiful. In verse 4 Paul says, "That every one of you should know how to possess his vessel in sanctification and honour." Now, I interpret the word vessel to mean "body." Some interpret it to mean "wife." According to the context, it seems to me that Paul is speaking about the body. He is saying, "Control your body."

Paul goes on to say "That no man go beyond and defraud his brother in any matter: because that the Lord is the avenger of all such, as we also have forewarned you and testified. For God hath not called us unto uncleanness, but unto holiness" (vv. 6-7). Now, what does the word *defraud* mean? Well, the word *fraud* means "to deceive." The word *fraud* means "to cheat." Integrity is the name of the game.

Paul wrote to the church at Corinth, "Come out from among them, and be ye separate, saith the Lord, and touch not the unclean thing; and I will receive you" (2 Corinthians 6:17). The psalmist wrote, "If I regard iniquity in my heart, the Lord will not hear me" (Psalm 66:18). Known and unconfessed sin in a believer's life blocks an understanding of God's will.

Again, in that familiar verse of Romans 12, the apostle Paul outlines the procedure for discovering God's will. After encouraging the believer to present his body as a sacrifice, Paul says, "and be not conformed to this world." I like the way J. B. Philips translates that verse: "Don't let the world around you squeeze you into its own mould" (Romans 12:2). Do not pattern yourself after the world around you.

John declared, "Love not the world, neither the things that are in the world. If any man love the world, the love of the Father is not in him" (1 John 2:15). James warned, "Whosoever . . . will be a friend of the world is the enemy of God" (James 4:4).

Obviously there is no way that we can remove all the influences of the world around us. Nor are we supposed to isolate ourselves from the world. The Bible says, in effect, the Christian must be *in* the world, but not *of* the world. We are not to accept or pursue the world's principles of living. We are to be a separated people.

What about it? Do you value God's will enough to turn your back on the pursuit of the world, the flesh, and the devil? You cannot, as Paul says, "prove" the perfect will of God if you are still "conformed to

this world." Remember the call is for transformers, not conformers. Do you really want to know God's will? Then may I urge you to deal first with the sin in your life. Why not pray:

> *Lord, in my heart today,*
> *I give Thee right of way,*
> *Work both to will and do*
> *And help me to be true.*

Sincerity

Fourth, if we are to know the will of God there must be more than just a head desire, there must be a burning, yearning, heart's desire to really experience God's way in our lives. This is confirmed by John 7:17. We could translate this verse, "If anyone wants to be doing His will, then he shall know about the teaching, whether it is from God or whether I am speaking from myself."

Yes, pine for thy God, fainting soul!
ever pine;

O languish mid all that life brings thee
   of mirth;
Famished, thirsty, and restless,—
   let such life be thine,—
For what sigh is to heaven, desire is
   to earth.

God loves to be longed for, He loves
   to be sought,
For He sought us Himself with such
   longing and love:
He died for desire of us, marvellous
   thought!
And he yearns for us now to be with
   Him above.

Frederick William Faber

Could it be that we are more concerned about getting God's OK on *our* plans than in having Jesus Christ show us *His* plans? Many people pray, "Lord, show me Thy will," when they really mean, "Lord, ease my conscience about what I've already done." Or else they say, "Lord, just give me an idea of what you have for me, and let me think about it." Friend, God does not reveal His will to let us toy with it.

Whatever bargaining tactic we may use, it amounts to placing our will *above* God's will. We are really reserving the right to make the final decision! But God's Word says that this is not acceptable. The Bible says we must be sincere or else forget it. We must seek the Lord, desire Him with all of our heart, and not be worried about our own interests and desires. And what does God's Word promise? "He shall direct thy paths" (Proverbs 3:6). What greater assurance could we ask for?

Do you want God's will? Then simply examine yourself, and do these four things God's Word prescribes:

1. Seek His forgiveness and receive the salvation that Jesus offers you.

2. Surrender your life wholly to Christ. Let Him be your *Lord,* as well as your Savior.

3. Separate yourself from the world. Stop pursuing its goals and seeking its pleasures.

4. Be sincere in your motives. Do not play games with God. Submit your desires to Him, and He will reveal His glorious will and plan for your life.

If you are right in these four areas, then do anything you want to do. You say, "What?" I said, "Do anything you want to do"; because, if you are right in these four areas, you will want God's glory only. Psalm 37:4 confirms this, "Delight thyself also in the LORD; and he shall give thee the desires of thine heart."

Yes, you can know the will of God today.

3

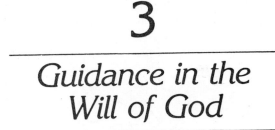

*Guidance in the
Will of God*

"And this is the confidence that we have in him, that, if we ask any thing accord-ing to his will, he heareth us: and if we know that he hear us, whatsoever we ask, we know that we have the petitions that we desired of him" (1 John 5:14-15).

"Study to shew thyself approved unto God, a workman that needeth not to be ashamed, rightly dividing the word of truth" (2 Timothy 2:15).

"And he that searcheth the hearts knoweth what is the mind of the Spirit, because he maketh intercession for the saints according to the will of God" (Romans 8:27).

"Trust in the LORD with all thine heart; and lean not unto thine own understand-ing. In all thy ways acknowledge him, and he shall direct thy paths" (Proverbs 3:5-6).

3

Guidance in the Will of God

Knowing God's will is the key to success in the Christian life. Dr. George Truett, a great Baptist preacher, put it this way: "To know the will of God is the greatest knowledge. To do the will of God is the greatest achievement." Truly it can be said that inside the will of God there is no failure. Outside the will of God there can be no real success. Knowing and obeying God's will is the key to any and all victory in the Christian's life!

"If this is true," you ask, "if knowing God's will is so important, what can I do to discover it? How can I know without doubt what God has planned for me?" Knowing God's will is not a mysterious thing. It takes no magic or psychic powers to discern what God wants you to do or where He wants you to go. For a Christian, finding God's will is really a very normal and natural thing. For the person who has surrendered himself to Jesus Christ, the will of God can be easily understood. Consider, for a moment, some of the various means of guidance we have in knowing the will of God.

The Bible

In the previous chapter, I stated that the will of God and the Word of God are inseparable. The Bible is our guidebook, our blueprint for dynamic living. Nowhere else can we find a more complete picture of God's will for man. As I mentioned before, much of God's will for you as an individual has already been given to you. You may not know what it is, but that is only because you have not taken the time to search for it in the Bible. Paul praised the believers in the city of Berea because, "they received the word [of God] with all readiness of mind, and searched the scriptures daily" (Acts 17:11).

Throughout the Bible there are literally hundreds of specific instructions, revelations of God's will that deal with many of the decisions we need to make. Whenever there is a matter of uncertainty in our minds, whenever we need to have a specific answer from the Lord, our first question should be, "What does God's Word have to say about this?"

We can rest assured that God's will and guidance for our lives will never contradict what He has already revealed to us in His written Word. God's will is always in perfect harmony with God's Word.

God speaks to us in the Bible. That is why He has given us this revelation of Himself. But an important principle to remember is that we *must* have a proper interpretation of God's Word in order to understand it, in order for it to make sense in our lives. Paul told Timothy, his son in the faith, "Study to shew thyself approved unto God, a workman that needeth not to be ashamed, rightly dividing the word of truth" (2 Timothy 2:15).

Some people treat the Bible like a magical formula. They dip in for a verse here and there, or they drop their Bible and let it fall open—thinking that God is going to give them some special instruction through a game of spiritual chance.

How foolish it is to treat God's Word this way! In his book, *God's Will For Your Life,* Dr. S. Maxwell Coder points out, "There is no doubt that God has often brought a certain verse to the attention of one of His children in an unusual and almost miraculous manner, for a special need, but the Word was never intended to be consulted in a superstitious manner."

Another principle to remember is that guidance that has to be squeezed and twisted out of God's Word is really no guidance at all. God will seldom, if ever, show His will to us if we try to force some truth from His Word. Too many people fail to realize that a proper interpretation of the Bible demands that we first study a passage in its proper context and then compare various passages to get a complete picture of God's principles. Lifting verses out of context and tailoring them

to suit our particular needs may bring us answers, but they will not be the right answers.

In his booklet, *Getting To Know the Will of God,* Dr. Alan Redpath tells that when he was trying to determine if God would have him enter the ministry, he made a list of all the arguments in favor of his staying in business. Each morning as he spent time in personal Bible study, he asked the Lord to show him particular verses that would counter each of the arguments he had written down. "Lord, I am not here to evade you," Redpath prayed. "I am here because I want to know your will. You saved me in order to guide and use me. Very well, then, Lord, what is your will?"

Alan Redpath relates:

Day by day I turned to my Bible. Almost every day a verse seemed to speak to me and I began to write that verse against one of the arguments. At the end of a year, every argument in favor of staying in business had been wiped out. It took over a year, but I was not in a hurry. I was willing to wait; I wanted it to be in God's time. Too much was at stake

*to dash into the thing. I wanted to in-
telligently find the will of God. And I
found it as I sought the Lord through my
daily reading and meditation. I commit-
ted it all to the Lord and step by step, the
way opened.*

Do you want to know God's will? Then
search for it first in the Bible. The
psalmist declared, "The entrance of thy
words *giveth light*" (Psalm 119:130). You
can have God's light shining in your life if
you will just turn on the power available in
His written Word.

Prayer

*The principal cause of my leanness and
unfruitfulness is owing to an unac-
countable backwardness to pray. I can*

write or read or converse or hear with a ready heart; but prayer is more spiritual and inward than any of these, and the more spiritual any duty is the more my carnal heart is apt to start from it.
Richard Newton

Another means of guidance in the will of God is prayer. In His Word God speaks to us. When we pray, we are talking to God. Communication is never possible unless there are two parties involved. Constant communication with our heavenly Father is vital if we truly want to know His plan for our lives. Someone has said, "Nothing lies beyond the reach of prayer except that which lies *outside* the will of God." As we study the Bible and as we study the history of the Church, we find that those men and women who truly accomplish great things *for* God were those who spent much time *with* God in prayer.

I have only missed my morning watch once or twice this term . . . I can easily believe that it is next in importance to accepting Christ. For I know that when I don't wait upon God in prayer and Bible study, things go wrong.
Borden of Yale

Paul Little tells that while still in college, he heard a speaker ask a question that changed his life. "How many of you who are concerned about the will of God," asked the man, "spend five minutes a day asking Him to show you His will?"

"It was," says Little, "as if somebody had grabbed me by the throat. At that time, I was . . . concerned about what I should do when I graduated from the university. I was running around campus, going to this meeting, reading that book, trying to find somebody's little formula.

. . . I was frustrated out of my mind, trying to figure out the will of God. I was doing everything but getting into the presence of God and asking Him to show me."

And Satan trembles when he sees
The weakest saint upon his knees.

What about you, friend? Are you concerned enough to spend as little as five minutes a day asking God to show you His will? It is interesting to note that after Paul's conversion on the road to Damascus, his first words were, "Lord, what wilt thou have me to do?" (Acts 9:6). Knowing God's will was his greatest pursuit. He wanted God's will more than life itself. Nothing should be allowed into our daily schedule that will crowd out our time alone with God.

I judge that my prayer is more than the devil himself, if it were otherwise I would have fared differently long before this. Yet men will not see and ac-knowledge the great wonders or miracles God works in my behalf. If I should neglect prayer but a single day, I should lose a great deal of the fire of faith.

Martin Luther

I know a great deal about my wife's in-terests. I know her likes and dislikes. I know what her favorite foods are, what kinds of books she likes to read, all about her. Why? Because I have spent many years in close communication with her. I have come to know her in an intimate and beautiful way. The closer we commune with our heavenly Father, the better we are going to know Him. The more time we spend in His presence, the less trouble we will have in determining His will. Prayer is a vital means of guidance into the will of God!

Hurry is the death of prayer.
Samuel Chadwick

Prayer is not something to be added after other approaches in our search for the will of God have been tried and have failed. No, we should pray as we use the personal resources God has given us.
T. B. Maston

The Work of the Holy Spirit
Closely related to the upward ministry of prayer is the inward working of the

Holy Spirit. Jesus told His disciples that when the Comforter, or the Holy Spirit, would come, He would guide them into all truth. One of the primary works of the Spirit in the Christian's life is to give wisdom and discernment—to demonstrate God's will. Paul declared, "As many as are led by the Spirit of God, they are the sons of God" (Romans 8:14). To the church at Philippi he wrote, "It is God which worketh in you both to will and to do of his good pleasure" (Philippians 2:13). God's Spirit is able to bring about the miraculous working of His will in our lives, but we must be willing to let Him have complete control and to be filled with the Spirit (Ephesians 5:18).

How does the Holy Spirit bring guidance in the Christian's life? Usually it is by an inward urging or compelling. In the book of Acts we find specific references to this compelling power. While Philip was busily engaged in a successful evangelistic campaign, the Holy Spirit spoke to him and said, "Arise and go toward the south . . . unto Gaza" (Acts 8:26). He was compelled to minister specifically to an Ethiopian who was hungry for God. Peter was led by the

Spirit to take the gospel of Christ to the house of Cornelius. Paul was directed by the Spirit to witness to the Macedonians. Hundreds of examples are given, in God's Word, of men who were directed by God's Spirit in specific ways. To the Child of God, the distinctive voice of the Holy Spirit can be just as clear and plain as if it were audible.

Normal Circumstances

Guidance in the will of God often comes to us in the normal circumstances and experiences of life. F. B. Meyer, the great English preacher, said: "When we want to know God's will, there are three things which always concur: the inward impulse, the Word of God and the trend of circumstances. . . . Never act until these three things agree."

Often the most obvious facts of life help us determine what God has and what He does not have for us. If, for instance, you find it difficult to carry even a simple tune, it is not likely that God would have you sing solos in your church! Gifts, abilities, aptitude—all are given to us to help us determine what our life's work should be.

But circumstances and the obvious facts of life should not be given more consideration than they deserve. Too often Christians become confused in their search for God's will because they make circumstances the primary factor in the decisions they make. God in His providence will place any number of stepping stones and stumbling blocks in our path. He will use the counsel and advice of friends and relatives. But He still expects us to be dependent upon Him. We should not rest solely upon our own experiences for guidance into His will. The ways in which God directs our lives are many, and the guidance which He gives to us is always good. The problem is that although God's transmitter is always in working condition, our receivers are sometimes faulty. Many times the signal from God, the indication of His will, is not picked up because our equipment is out of order.

Do you want to know God's will? Then be very sure that your life is in working condition. Be careful to meditate in God's Word daily and to spend time in prayer. Be sensitive to the inward voice of the

Holy Spirit and to the everyday experiences God brings your way.

James declared, "If any of you lack wisdom [need to know the will of God], let him ask of God . . . and it shall be given him" (James 1:5). God is deeply interested *in* you. He has a glorious plan and purpose *for* you. And He wants to share it *with* you.

Six Steps to Knowing God's Will

(1) I seek at the beginning to get my heart into such a state that it has no will of its own in regard to a given matter. Nine-tenths of the trouble with people is just here. Nine-tenths of the difficulties are overcome when our hearts are ready to do the Lord's will, whatever it may be. When one is truly in this state, it is usually but a little way to the knowledge of what His will is.

90

(2) Having done this, I do not leave the result to feeling or simple impression. If I do so, I make myself liable to great delusions.

(3) I see the will of the Spirit of God through, or in connection with, the Word of God. The Spirit and the Word must be combined. If I look to the Spirit alone without the Word, I lay myself open to great delusions also. If the Holy Spirit guides us at all, He will do it according to the Scriptures and never contrary to them.

(4) Next I take into account providential circumstances. These often plainly indicate God's will in connection with His Word and Spirit.

(5) I ask God in prayer to reveal His will to me aright.

(6) Thus, through prayer to God, the study of the Word, and reflection, I come to a deliberate judgment according-ing to the best of my ability and knowledge; and if my mind is thus at peace, and continues so after two or three more petitions, I proceed accord-ingly. In trivial matters, and in trans-actions involving more important issues, I have found this method always effective.

George Mueller*

---

*As quoted from S. Maxwell Coder, *God's Will for Your Life* (Chicago: Moody, 1946), pp. 79-80.

4

You Can Be Happy in God's Will

"The God of our fathers hath chosen thee, that thou shouldest know his will, and see that Just One, and shouldest hear the voice of his mouth. For thou shalt be his witness unto all men of what thou hast seen and heard" (Acts 22:14-15).

"Or what man is there of you, whom if his son ask bread, will he give him a stone? Or if he ask a fish, will he give him a serpent? If ye then, being evil, know how to give good gifts unto your children, how much more shall your Father which is in heaven give good things to them that ask him?" (Matthew 7:9-11).

"Thy kingdom come. Thy will be done in earth, as it is in heaven" (Matthew 6:10).

"For I came down from heaven, not to do mine own will, but the will of him that sent me" (John 6:38).

"And he went a little farther, and fell on his face, and prayed, saying, O my Father, if it be possible, let this cup pass from me: nevertheless not as I will, but as thou wilt" (Matthew 26:39).

"Trust in the Lord *with all thine heart; and lean not unto thine own understanding. In all thy ways acknowledge him, and he shall direct thy paths" (Proverbs 3:5-6).*

4

You Can Be Happy in God's Will

No one should ever be afraid of God's will.

Unfortunately, there are some people today who feel that the will of God is always unpleasant. They are afraid to submit to God's purpose, because they are sure that happiness and God's will cannot be compatible. They spend most of their life trying to avoid God's plan, thinking the will of God will somehow make them unhappy.

But according to the Bible, nothing could be further from the truth. The Bible tells us that when we delight ourselves in the Lord—when we allow Him to have control of our lives—He will give us the desires of our hearts (Psalm 37:4).

In the three preceding chapters we have examined why it is important that we know God's will, we have tried to define what God's will really is, and we have looked at some of the ways in which God reveals His will to us. In this chapter, I would like to consider three important truths related to knowing God's will.

1. *God wants us to be happy in His will!*

God is no Scrooge! He is not a stern dictator who is always trying to crack the whip over our heads.

Some people seem to think, says Paul Little, that "God peers over the balcony of heaven trying to find anybody who is enjoying life. And when He spots a happy person, He yells, 'Now cut that out!' That concept of God should make us shudder because it's blasphemous!"

God wants His very best for you. Do you believe that? He wants your life to hold a definite purpose, and He wants you to enjoy life to its fullest. In fact, God is far more concerned that we enjoy ourselves than we are! That sounds incredible, but it is absolutely true. Often, though, the things that we think will bring happiness are really not what is best for us.

There are many harmful pleasures in life. There is the lustful pleasure that is promoted in much of today's literature and in the media. This is the kind of pleasure that is self-seeking, that desires fleshly gratification.

It is true that sinful activity brings some sort of pleasure. Satan is no fool; he makes sin not only attractive, but enjoyable as well. But this kind of pleasure is not lasting. It may taste good going down, but it leaves a bitter aftertaste in the mouth. It also enslaves us, and we become addicted to it, desiring more and more all the time.

Some people act as if God were out to reform them, to take all their pleasures away. But what He really wants is to direct us into that true pleasure that brings lasting fulfillment and satisfaction. When

we seek God's will, we find that He helps us make the right decisions. He opens and closes the doors that will lead us in the right direction. He shapes our interests and desires so that we will not stumble and fall into the pitfalls along the way.

Has it ever occurred to you that you could be much happier if you would stop trying to run things your own way, and would let Christ have complete control of your life? God's will is that you and I be happy! There is absolutely no reason to be afraid of His direction in our lives. Remember, Paul wrote to the Christians at Rome of "that *good,* and *acceptable,* and [even more, that] *perfect,* will of God" (Romans 12:2). This is what God wants for us.

We all at times, says Paul Little, make the mistake of thinking that our choice is between "doing what we want to do and being happy, and doing what God wants us to do and being miserable." There is always that feeling that maybe God is going to shortchange us. Let me say again, nothing could be further from the truth!

Dr. Oswald Hoffman has said, "Having given us the package, do you think God will deny us the ribbon?" How ridiculous!

God does not give us a new life in Christ and then try to make us miserable in it.

Jesus raised a similar question one day as He spoke to His disciples. "What man is there of you, whom if his son ask bread, will he give him a stone? Or if he ask a fish, will he give him a serpent? If ye then, being evil, know how to give good gifts unto your children, *how much more* shall your Father which is in heaven give good things to them that ask him?" (Matthew 7:9-11).

Most of us are inclined to give our chidren too much—sometimes more than is good for them. Why? Because we love them! They are our own flesh and blood, and we want to show our affection for them.

Jesus was simply saying, in Matthew 7, "Don't you think that your heavenly Father, who is the personification of all that is good, is able to give you much greater things? Don't you realize that He is much more concerned about you than you are about your own children?" God the Father loves you, God the Son died for you, and God the Holy Spirit indwells each believer forever. The Trinity is for you. He who has created us and sustains us from day to day is not going to make us unhappy if we accept His will. He wants what is best for us. God wants us to be happy in His will.

2. *God's will does not have to be contrary to ours!*

Some people become very alarmed whenever they have a strong desire to do anything, because they are convinced that if they want something badly, it cannot possibly be God's will for them.

I remember counseling a young man, some time ago, who was very depressed because the greatest desire he had in life was to become a doctor. Despite the fact that his interests, aptitude, and educational background all indicated that he was ideally suited for this profession, he was sure it must not be God's will, because he wanted it so much.

But wait a minute! Didn't we already say that God wants us to be happy? Isn't God desirous of giving us what is best? Doesn't Paul describe God's will as that which is *good* and *acceptable*? Why do we so often demonstrate this kind of mistrust? Why can't we take God at His Word and rely on Him to lead us and give us the right desires and ambitions?

David said, "Delight thyself . . . in the LORD; and he shall give thee the desires of thine heart. Commit thy way unto the LORD; trust also in him; and he shall bring it to pass" (Psalm 37:4-5). Solomon was told to ask God for whatever he wanted. And when he made his request, it was granted. Don't you suppose that if God urged Solomon to choose, and then honored that choice, that He wishes us to do the same thing? Remember, God is for us (Romans 8:31).

It is not a difficult matter to learn what it means to delight ourselves in the Lord. It is to live so as to please Him, to honor everything we find in His Word, to do everything the way He would like to have it done, and for Him.

S. Maxwell Coder

In an article entitled "How to Know God's Will" (*Letters of Interest,* January 1969), William Anderson said:

> There was a dispensation in which God made most of the decisions for His people. Paul describes it (in his letter to the church at Galatia) as the time when God's people were little children under the custody of the law. All the details were spelled out for them; they were like slaves. "But," Paul insists, ". . . thou art no more a servant, but a son" (Galatians 4:7). Times have changed. And a son is not under the detailed regulations of law.
>
> The whole concept of life nowadays is different from that of the Old Testament. It is the difference between the immaturity of children and the maturity of sons. Those who wish God to regulate every detail and make every decision are really hankering after the old slavery of a past age. They refuse the freedom and responsibilities of sons.

God does not want to dictate His will to

you. He wants you to have the liberty of a mature child of God. We are not to be robots, incapable of or afraid of taking initiative, but mature believers with the divine wisdom and discernment to make the right decisions.

If a Christian is daily spending time in God's Word and in prayer, if he is maturing and growing in his relationship with the Lord, he is going to have that maturity he needs to make the right choices. And *his* will, will coincide with *God's* will.

Occasionally we talk about being in the center of God's will, as if that center were an exact pinpoint. At times it certainly may be, but Kenneth Pike suggests, "Perhaps some of our teaching about [God's will] could be made more helpful if we supplemented it by additional figures of speech. It is useful . . . for example, to think of God's will as an area in a television wave guide or tube. As I understand it, the waves in this tube bounce back and forth anywhere within the tube that they 'want' to go, completely free so long as they remain in the tube. They are not channeled to a thin line—they just can't go outside of the wave guide." They have freedom to choose—but it is a freedom of discipline and order. It is a freedom within specific and definite boundaries. And that is the way it is with you and me.

God's will does not have to be contrary to ours. We are given the freedom of choice. And as A. W. Tozer said, "The man or woman who is wholly or joyously surrendered to Christ, can't make a wrong choice—any choice will be the right one."

———————◆———————

3. *Living in God's will is the only way to be successful in the Christian life!*

The greatest illustration of conforming to the will of God is seen in Jesus Christ. His entire life was one of submission to God the Father. Jesus plainly said, "I came down from heaven, not to do mine own will, but the will of him that sent me" (John 6:38). On another occasion Jesus said, "My meat is to do the will of him that sent me, and to finish his work" (John 4:34). He taught His followers to pray, "Thy will be done in earth, as it is in heaven" (Matthew 6:10). As Jesus in Gethsemane's garden contemplated the cross, He prayed, "Father, if thou be willing, remove this cup from me: nevertheless, not my will, but thine, be done" (Luke 22:42). The complete life of Jesus was one of perfect submission to the will of God. Yes, and we too can conform to the will of God through the power of the indwelling Holy Spirit.

Just as the waves in the television tube cannot go outside the wave guide, so we must not go outside God's will for our life if we want to realize the plan and purpose God has for us. We cannot expect to deliberately ignore the revealed will and Word of God and be happy. It just will not work! Knowing God's purpose is not a take-it-or-leave-it option for the child of God. Paul commands us to understand what the will of the Lord is (Ephesians 5:17). *Discovering the will of God is an imperative!* It is just as important, perhaps more important, than any of the other commands in the Bible.

As long as we are in God's will, in His "wave guide," we are going to experience God's blessing. As long as we are obeying His Word and yielding to the Holy Spirit within us, we will be successful.

In a recent study of hurricanes, the United States Weather Service decided to fly some men into the very center of a storm to study its effect. To their amazement, they discovered that at the very eye of a hurricane there is a complete calm —no wind at all! For the Christian surrounded by turmoil, engulfed in the conflicts of life, that same peace and calm is available. It is found in the center of God's will.

The psalmist taught that the person who discovers true blessing, true happiness, walks not with the ungodly, but *delights* himself in the law of the Lord. "Whatsoever he doeth shall prosper" (Psalm 1:3).

5

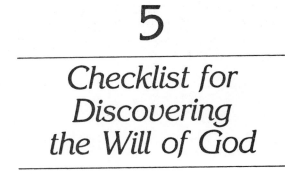

Checklist for
Discovering
the Will of God

5

Checklist for Discovering the Will of God

Repeatedly the Bible encourages believers in Jesus Christ to know and do the will of God. "Be ye not unwise, but understanding what the will of the Lord is" (Ephesians 5:17). God has a plan for your life. May I challenge you to wholeheartedly seek that plan?

Here is a review checklist that may help you—eight steps in discovering the will of God:

1. Be sure of your personal salvation.

"The Lord is not slack concerning his promise, as some men count slackness; but is longsuffering to us-ward, not willing that any should perish, but that all should come to repentance" (2 Peter 3:9).

God's will is that we be His children, and until we are born of God, He cannot lead us as a father leads his children. Until we are converted, we can have little part in God's divine plan and purpose. It is God's will that men be saved.

Have you taken this very first step in the will of God?

2. Surrender your life completely to Jesus Christ.

The Bible points out that it is impossible for us to see further into God's will unless we are willing to obey that which

114

we have already seen. We are told, "Be ye not unwise, but understanding what the will of the Lord is" (Ephesians 5:17). Another word for "unwise" is *foolish*. It is foolish to neglect the will of God.

"I beseech you therefore, brethren, by the mercies of God, that ye present your bodies a living sacrifice, holy, acceptable unto God, which is your reasonable service. And be not conformed to this world: but be ye transformed by the renewing of your mind, that ye may prove what is that good, and acceptable, and perfect, will of God" (Romans 12:1-2).

To present your body as a "living sacrifice" means full, enthusiastic obedience to God's will. Continual obedience is essential.

3. *Live a life that is separated from the world.*

It is obviously God's will that believers know a great deal about holy living.

"For this is the will of God, even your sanctification, that ye should abstain from fornication. . . . For God hath not

115

called us unto uncleanness, but unto holiness" (1 Thessalonians 4:3, 7).

The call today is for transformers rather than conformers. Why not pray:

> *Lord, in my heart today,*
> *I give Thee right of way,*
> *Work both to will and do*
> *And help me to be true.*

4. Be sure you are sincere.

"If any man will do his will, he shall know of the doctrine, whether it be of God, or whether I speak of myself" (John 7:17).

If we are to discover God's will, there must be more than a casual desire; there must be a sincere yearning to experience all that God has for us.

5. Search the Scriptures for God's will.

It is essential to understand that the will of God and the Word of God are insep-arable. The major portion of God's will for your life has already been given in the Word of God.

"Trust in the LORD with all thine heart; and lean not unto thine own understanding. In all thy ways acknowledge him, and he shall direct thy paths" (Proverbs 3:5-6).

Throughout the Bible there are many commands that tell us what to do and what not to do. Where there is no direct, clear teaching on a subject, we are encouraged to seek biblical principles.

Do you know God's will? I challenge you to diligently examine the Word of God.

"The entrance of thy words giveth light; it giveth understanding unto the simple" (Psalm 119:130).

6. *Communicate with God in prayer.*

"And this is the confidence that we have in him, that, if we ask any thing according to his will, he heareth us: and if we know that he hear us, whatsoever we ask, we know that we have the petitions that we desired of him" (1 John 5:14-15).

In the Bible, God speaks to us. When

117

we pray, we speak to God. Communication is never possible unless there are two parties involved. Are you concerned enough to spend as little as five minutes a day asking God to show you His will?

The more we commune with our heavenly Father, the better we are going to know Him and determine His will.

7. *Pay attention to the leading of the Holy Spirit.*

"For as many as are led by the Spirit of God, they are the sons of God" (Romans 8:14).

Closely related to the upward ministry of prayer is the inward working of the Holy Spirit.

How does the Holy Spirit guide us? Usually it is by an inward compelling. Hundreds of examples are given in the Bible of men and women who were directed into a particular sphere of activity by the urging of the Holy Spirit. To the child of God, His voice can and should be clear.

8. *Look for God's guidance in the normal*

circumstances of life and the counsel of spiritual friends.

"For a great door and effectual is opened unto me, and there are many adversaries" (1 Colossians 16:9).

Often guidance in the will of God will come to us in the normal circumstances of life, through open and closed doors. But be careful not to give this area more consideration than it deserves. Satan can also open and shut doors of opportunity. Gather all the facts, and prayerfully seek the mind of God.

At times the advice of parents, a pastor, or Christian friends can be of great help. Seek their advice but not their leading. There is no substitute for real, unbroken communion with God.

"Where no counsel is, the people fall: but in the multitude of counsellors there is safety" (Proverbs 11:14).

Remember always that the Lord is deeply interested in you. He has a satisfying plan and purpose for your life. You can discover God's will!

"The God of our fathers hath chosen thee, that thou shouldest know his will" (Acts 22:14).